W9-BGH-030

Dear Lord

by

Bill Adler

publishers since 1798

THOMAS NELSON, PUBLISHERS
Nashville • Camden • New York

Published in Nashville, Tennessee, by Thomas Nelson, Inc., Publishers and distributed in Canada by Lawson Falle, Ltd., Cambridge, Ontario.

Printed in the United States of America.

Illustrated by Bettye Beach

ISBN 0-8407-5266-0

Dear Lord

Pear LORD,

    I hope you listen to my prayers because I have a lot to say.

        Sincerely yours,
        Robert
        Age 7 Evansville

Dear Lord,
Thank you for making
today a nice day.
Thank you for making
tomorrow a nice day even
if it isn't tomorrow yet.
Yours truly
Susan
Age 7
Cherry Hill

Dear Lord,

Please take care of everybody in the whole world Except the land lord.

I love you
Gwen
Age 8
Indianapolis

Dear Lord,

I need a raise in my allowance. Could you have one of your angels tell my father.

Thank you

David
Age 7
Durham

Dear Lord,

Please take care of my dog Little Red. He is sick and he can't pray for himself because he is only a dog.

Love,
Marsha
Age 8
Bridgewater

Deer Lord,

    Please help me in school.
I need help in speling. addin
historie, geografy and writin
I do not need help in
    enything else
      Lois
      Age 9
    San Bernadino

Dear Lord,

I am saying this prayer for my grandmother.

She is very old and sick and I hope she gets better soon so she can watch the soap operas on television again which she loves the most after me and my mom.

Your friend
Peter
Age 9
New Milford

Dear Lord,

Please answer my prayers. Even if I am just a kid.

MICHAEL
Age 8
Lake City

Dear Lord,

Please help my mother to lose weight.

She is on a diet and she is trying very hard but sometimes she eats chocolate cake and ice cream.

That is why she needs your help. My mother would pray for your help but she is too embarrassed.

Love
Stephanie
Age 9
Gadsden

Dear Lord,

Tonight I am standing when I say my prayers because my mother just bougnt me new pajamas and I dorit want to get them dirty.

Jonathan

Age 8

Virginia Beach

Dear Lord,

Could you please send our family some money? I know you aren't supposed to pray for money but we are very poor.

I hope you aren't mad that I asked for the money.

Your friend,
Bess
Age 9
Ann Arbor

Dear Lord

Do you love
every body? Even
little boys who get into
a lot of trubble?
Mark
Age 6
Savannah

Dear Lord

I say my prayers every
ight before I go to bed.
(after I watch STAR TREK)

Your friend

Stevie

Age 8

Farmingdale

Dear Lord

I would like to be tall. I am the shortest kid in my class and they all call me pee wee.

I don't want to be pee wee anymore.

Neil

Age 9

Eugene

dear Lord,

I am praying for a new stove
for my mother. The stove she's got
Cant Cook so good.

Yours truly,

Annie

Age 8
Scottsdale

Dear Lord,

Please help my father get a new job. The job he's got makes him sick and tired

Thank you

Love

Cynthia

Age 7

Pensacola

Dear Lord,
    Thank you for the
nice day today.
    You even fooled the T.V.
weatherman.

                Hank
                Age 7
                Pontotoc

Dear LORD,

Tomorrow is my birthday
Could you please put a
rainbow in
the sky?

Love,
Susan

Age 9
Chicago

dear Lord,

I am praying for all the poor people in the world I am one of the poor people.

I only get 25¢ a week allowance.

Sincerely,
Gary
Age 8
Harrisburg

dear Lord,

Bless this house.
And all who live here.
Bless this house, and
my grandmother who
used to live here and is
now in heaven, I think.

Love,
Caroline
Age 7
Wichita Falls

Dear Lord,

My mother has a bad headache again today. Can you help her with her headache?

When she has a headache, she is in a bad mood and then my father gets a headache, too.

Joseph

Age 9

Houston

Dear Lord,
   Say hello to the angels for me.
   Grandma says I am an angel too.
                Betsy
                Age 5
                Menomonee Falls

deer Lord,

Please stop the snow.
It snowed all week
and everybody is sick of snow,
espeicially the kids who have
to clean the driveway
like me.

William
Age 9
Duluth

Dear Lord,

Bless my house
And bless my parents.
Bless my sister
And my new puppy.
Bless my Aunt Sarah
And my Uncle Jack
And bless our new Color
T.v. set so it doesn't break
like the old one.

Love, Martin
Age 9
Atlanta

Dear Lord,

Thank you Lord, for the best mother and father in the world. And thank you, Lord, for my brother.

He is not the best brother in the whole world but he is the only brother I have.

Love,
Jennifer
Age 8
Brunswick

dear lord.

I am 7.

I don't know much.
Please help me to be smart
when I am 8.
Carl
Age 7
Booneville

Dear Lord,

How do I know that you hear my prayers?

Could you please give me a sign like leaving me a $10 bill under my pillow.

Gloria

Age 10

Forest Park

Dear Lord,

I am praying for the President of the USA because he is too busy to pray because he has to watch out for the whole country.

even the people who didn't vote for him.

Sincerely,
Arthur

Age 9
Alexandria

dear Lord,

I won't pray too long because I know a lot of the other kids want to pray to you.

Please listen to their prayers too except Michael.

He only prays when he is in trouble which is every day.

Yours truly,

Natalie

Age 8

Hartford

Deer LORD,

I am saying my prayers for me and my brother Billy because Billy is 6 months old and he can't do anything but sleep and wet his diapers.

Yours truly,
Diane

Age 8   St. Charles

Dear Lord,

I have been a good girl and I help my mother with the dishes and I throw out the garbage and I walk the dog and I brush my teeth everyday and I go to church every Sunday.

I hope I will go to Heaven some day because I don't want to be good for nothing.

Your friend
Claudia
Age 8
Boise

Dear LORD,

I say my prayers every night before I go to sleep even if I don't want a new doll or fire engine.

Susan
Age 7
Anaheim

Dear Lord,

My father died last year and we need a new daddy. Please help my mom to find one.

Love,
Stella
Age 10
Goshen

Dear LORD,

Thank-you for taking care of me and my family. I hope you will take care of us again next year if you aren't too tired.

Sincerely yours
Mickey
Age 7
Philadelphia

dear Lord,

   My tooth came out and I put it under my pillow for the tooth fairy.

   Would you please tell her it iz there.

From
Lowell
Age 7
Chicopee Fallz

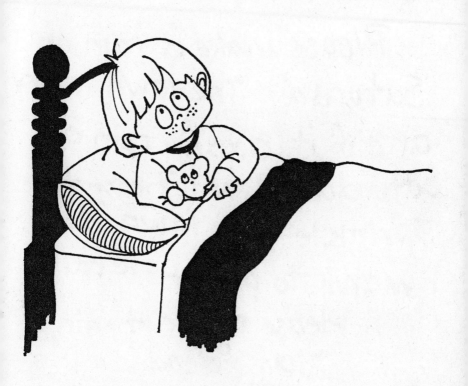

Dear Lord,

Please make it rain on Saturday. The lawn is dry and if it doesn't rain on Saturday, I will have to sprinkle the lawn and I want to play baseball.

Please make it rain.

Your friend
Steve
Age 9
Meridian

Dear Lord,

I hope you get my letter. Do you have a post office in heaven?

From

Jeanne

Age 7

Seattle

Dear Lord,

I am 8

I would like to go to heaven and shake your hand.

Billy
Age 8
Amarillo

Dear LORd,

I hope you can hear my prayers because it is very noisy in my room.

My brother has the TV set on.

Jimmy
Age 7
St. Albans

Dear Lord,

How old are you?
Are you a million years old? I bet you are the oldest person in the whole world.

Bruce
Age 8
Cedar City

Dear Lord,
  Do dogs go to heaven
I hope so.
  Our dog. Skipper died and
I hope he doesn't go to
the other place. Love
                Barbara
Tallahasee   Age 6

Dear Lord,

Please take care of my mother, my father, my grandmother, my grandfather, my uncle, my aunt, my cousin, my sister, my brother, my friends, my minister my teacher and anybody else I forgot.

Johnny
Age 8
Coffeyville

Dear Lord.

Could you please send one of your angels to help my mother around the house. She has a lot of work to do and she is always tired. My daddy helps sometimes when he isn't sleeping on the couch.

Laura
Age 8
Pikeville

Dear Lord,

I love you a lot even if you don't help me pass my arithmetic test.

Jeffrey
Age 7
Brewster

Dear Lord.
I am a good Christian. I go to church every Sunday except when I have to play Little League baseball.
Stanley
Age 8
Coopers Plains

dear Lord,

Do you have a long white beard?

My grandfather said you have a long white beard and I think he knows you.

Gwen
Age 8
Tyler

Dear LORD,
This is my prayer.
Could you please give my
brother some brains.
So far he doesn't have
any.

Angela
Age 8

Dear <u>Lord</u>,

Please make me better.
I have a bad stomackache
from too much candy
again.

Yours truly
Lucy
Age 7
Portland

dear lord,

Nobody knows what you look like.

I drew a picture of you.

Now everybody knows what you look like.

Jamie

Age 7

Medina

Dear Lord,
   I say my prayers
3 times a day because
I don't want to take
any chances.
         Sincerely,
         Mike
         Age 7
         Philadelphia

Dear Lord,

How many angels are there in heaven? I would like to be the first kid in my class to know the answer.

Norma
Age 8
Dubuque

Dear Lord,
   Now I Lay me down to sleep
I pray the lord my soul to keep.
And if I should die before
       I wake,
I pray my brother doesn't
   get all my good
       toys.
           Roger
           Age 8
           Memphis

Dear Lord,
  please send a new baby
for Mommy. The new
baby you sent last
week cries _too much_.

Love,
Debbie
Age 7
Coral Gables

Dear Lord,
I have been a good boy all year except sometimes when I'm not.
Sincerely
Mickey
Age 10
Albany

Dear Lord,

Do you listen to everybody's prayers every night?

If you do, you don't have time to do anything else like taking care of the world.

David
Age 8
Jamestown

Dear Lord

How long have you been in heaven?

We have lived in this house for two years.

Ethel

Age 8

Steubenville

Dear Lord,

Please take good care of my baby sister. She is only one and she can't even cross the street by herself yet.

Love,
Bernice
Age 7
Brooklyn

Dear Lord,

Are there any good Christians in Washington?

Sincerely,
Harriet
Age 8
Lynchburg

dear Lord,

Why do you have to brush your teeth every day to be a good Christian?

My mother says you do.

Love,
Arthur
Age 7
Irwin

Dear Lord,
   Please bring me a new brother. The one I got socks me all the time.
   Love,
   David
   Age 6
   Shreveport

Dear Lord,

Do you have any helpers in Heaven? I would like to be one of your helpers in Heaven when I have summer vacation.

Sincerely,

Mary

Age 10

Joplin

Dear Lord,
Will I have my own room in heaven? I am 7 and I sleep in the same room with my brother and two sisters.

Mark
Age 7
Pittsburg

Dear Lord,

Please send me your picture. I will put it next to my picture of Elvis.

Love,
Bonnie
Age 8
Cairo

Dear Lord,

I say prayers every night except when I have an upset stomach and I don't want to talk to anybody.

Teddy
Age 8

Anniston

Dear Lord,
  Do you have any
favorite Christians?
    I would like to
be one.
        Love
        Mary
        Age 8
        Anderson

Dear Lord,

Do you ever get mad.

My mother gets mad all the time but she is only a human.

Yours truly
David
Age 8
Stanford

Dear Lora,

We need some rain.

Could you cry a little so we can get some rain?

Robin
Age 6
Medina

Dear LORD,

I Read your book The Bible and I liked it a lot except for ~~for~~ some of the big words.

Heather

Age 7

Wilmington

Dear Lord.
   Sometimes I say my
prayers in the morning
because I can't say my prayers
at night because I have to
brush my teeth and wash my
face and hands and I'm very
busy.
                Yours truly
                   Joan
                Age 7
             Nashville

Dear Lord,

Do you take care of cats?

My cat is called Kitty and Kitty says her prayers every night.

Love,
Stephanie
Age. 7
Wa shoe.

Dear lord,

Do you ever get mad? My mother says God never gets mad except when children don't do their homework.

Your friend,
Larry
Age 7   Frankfort

Dear Lord,

    I would like to be your helper when I grow up.

      Stephen
      Age 9
      Chicago

P.S. You don't have to pay me.

Dear Lord,
Were you a
Person before you
Were God?

Holly
Age 5
Stanford

Dear Lord,

My grandma just went to heaven. Please take care of her.

Her name is Grandma.

Your Christian.

Paul

Age 7

Cincinnati

Bill Adler's "letter" books have total sales of over two million copies. The collection includes such best sellers as *Dear Pastor, Letters from Camp, Kid's Letters to President Kennedy,* and more than twenty-five others. Mr. Adler lives in New York City.